BUSINESS/SCIENCE/TECHNOLOGY DIVISION
CHICAGO PUBLIC LIBRARY
400 SOUTH STATE STREET
CHICAGO, IL 60605

Your Book of Veteran and Edwardian Cars

The YOUR BOOK Series

- Acting
- Aeromodelling
- Animal Drawing
- Aquaria
- Astronomy
- Athletics
- Basketball
- Bird Watching
- Bridges
- Butterflies and Moths
- Camping
- Canoeing
- The Way a Car Works
- Card Games
- Chemistry
- Chess
- Coin Collecting
- Computers
- Confirmation
- Contract Bridge
- Cricket
- Diving
- The Earth
- Electronics
- Embroidery
- Engines and Turbines
- The English Bible
- The English Church
- Fencing
- Figure Drawing
- Flower Making
- Flying
- Freshwater Life
- Furniture
- Golf
- Gymnastics
- Heraldry
- Hockey
- Hovercraft
- The Human Body
- Judo
- Kites
- Knitting and Crochet
- Knots
- Landscape Drawing
- Light
- Lino-cutting
- Magic
- Maps and Map Reading
- Medieval and Tudor Costume
- Model Car Racing
- Model Railways
- Modelling
- Money
- Music
- Netball
- Nineteenth Century Costume
- Paper Folding
- Parliament
- Party Games
- Patience
- Pet Keeping
- Photographing Wild Life
- Photography
- Keeping Ponies
- Puppetry
- The Recorder
- Rugger
- The Seashore
- Self-Defence
- 17th & 18th Century Costume
- Sewing
- Shell Collecting
- Skating
- Soccer
- Sound
- Space Travel
- Squash
- Stamps
- Surnames
- Survival Swimming and Life Saving
- Swimming
- Table Tennis
- Tape Recording
- Television
- Tennis
- Trampolining
- Trees
- Underwater Swimming
- Veteran and Edwardian Cars
- Vintage Cars
- Watching Wild Life
- Waterways
- Weather
- Weaving
- Wild Flowers
- Woodwork
- The Year

Your Book of
Veteran and Edwardian Cars

by

John Coleman

with drawings by Harry Tucker

FABER & FABER
3 Queen Square
London

*First published in 1971
by Faber and Faber Limited
3 Queen Square London WC1
Printed in Great Britain by
Latimer Trend & Co Ltd Plymouth
All rights reserved*

ISBN 0 571 09375 2

© *John Coleman
1971*

Contents

1. Introduction	*page* 11
2. The Birth of the Motor Car in Germany	15
3. France—the Cradle of the Motor Car	20
4. The Handicapped Beginnings of British Motoring	26
5. The Edwardian Era on the Continent	38
6. Separate Development in the U.S.A.	42
7. Brooklands and the Dawn of Motor Racing	47
8. A Final Survey of the Edwardian Scene	52
9. Museums, Clubs and Events You Should Know About	55
Some Other Books to Read	58
Index	61

Illustrations

PLATES

Between pages 48 and 49

1. 3½ h.p. Benz of 1898 accompanied by tricycle of the period (*Montagu Motor Museum*)
2. The first four-wheeled Daimler of 1886 (*Montagu Motor Museum*)
3. The first Benz motorized tricycle of 1885 (*Montagu Motor Museum*)
4. Close-up view of the Benz engine (*Montagu Motor Museum*)
5. 1901 Mercedes (*Montagu Motor Museum*)
6. 1894 Panhard (*Science Museum*)
7. A 1901 Benz in the 1931 Brighton Run (*Montagu Motor Museum*)
8. Butler's Petrol-cycle displayed with specifications (*Science Museum*)
9. Lord Montagu's father taking King Edward VII (then Prince of Wales) for the first royal drive in a German-built 12 h.p. Daimler
10. 1897 Lanchester (*Science Museum*)
11. The original Rolls-Royce Silver Ghost (*Rolls-Royce*)
12. 1905 Wolseley designed by Herbert Austin (*British Leyland Motor Corporation*)
13. Assembling the first Rover car in 1904 (*Rover Co.*)
14. Two early Standard cars of 1908 and 1907 (*J. R. Davy*)

Illustrations

15. Percy Riley's tricar of 1904 (*Science Museum*)
16. 1913 Morgan (*Science Museum*)
17. Mr. and Mrs. Henry Ford in the first Ford car of 1896 (*Montagu Motor Museum*)
18. Henry Ford in Model A (*Ford Motor Company*)
19. Early assembly line for the flywheel-magneto of the Model T (*Ford Motor Company*)
20. Gordon Crosby painting of S. F. Edge's successful attempt at the 24 hour record in 1907 (*The Autocar*)
21. 120 h.p. Itala (*Montagu Motor Museum*)
22. 1908 Grand Prix Austin (*Montagu Motor Museum*)
23. 15 h.p. Austin 'Ascot' two-seater phaeton (*Montagu Motor Museum*)
24. A British Daimler of around 1911 (*V. H. Mant*)

25 and 26. 1913 Chater-Lea, showing condition before and after repair (*Charlie Russett*)

27. William Morris seated at the wheel of his first Bullnose Morris (*British Leyland Motor Corporation*)

Illustrations

LINE DRAWINGS

1. Nicolas Joseph Cugnot's steam carriage	*page*	11
2. The car made by Siegfried Marcus in 1874		15
3. Close view of the tiller steering on the 1885 Benz		17
4. 'L'Obéissante', the steam carriage built by Bollée in 1873		20
5. Louis Renault at the wheel of his first car		23
6. 1903 de Dion Bouton		24
7. 1895 Knight		27
8. 1904 7 h.p. Alldays and Onions		29
9. 1909 7 h.p. Austin car of Swift design		33
10. 1907 16/20 h.p. Sunbeam		33
11. One of Vauxhall's first cars 1903/4		34
12. 1906 6 h.p. Calthorpe		35
13. The A.C. Sociable 1909		36
14. 20/30 h.p. Renault of 1906		38
15. The Bébé Peugeot of 1912		39
16. 1911 27 h.p. Delaunay-Belleville		40
17. Type 13 Bugatti		41
18. 1893 Duryea		42
19. Model T Ford of 1909		43
20. The 'Curved Dash' Oldsmobile		45
21. 1912 Turner		52
22. 45 h.p. Napier Pullman		53

1 · *Introduction*

Perhaps the most amazing thing about the Motor Car is the vast expanse of time during which it did not exist at all. The Chinese, the Egyptians, the Greeks, the Romans—through all these great and ingenious civilizations automotive power was never more than a dream in the minds of a few extraordinary men who faintly perceived that it *could* exist. The Greeks invented a kind of steam engine but only the 'puff' of the steam was used to drive it and it had no real power; it was a matter of using steam like the wind to drive a miniature windmill. It was not until the great inventors of the steam age, Thomas Newcomen, James Watt and George Stephenson, came along that the *captive* power of steam was at long last realized. The idea of an engine to drive a moving vehicle became a real possibility and soon the *Rocket* and other powerful locomotives were in existence. It was obvious that attempts should be made to adapt this amazing new form of power to road vehicles, to make it take the place of the horse to pull carts and carriages. The first successful attempt in this direction was the famous steam carriage made by Nicolas Joseph Cugnot in 1769. To us today it must seem pretty obvious that the great

1. Difficulties with the steering of Nicolas Joseph Cugnot's steam carriage

Introduction

boiler which swung round with the steering mechanism of the single front wheel was bound to make the vehicle hopelessly unstable and we are not surprised to hear that the first of Cugnot's carriages ran into a brick wall and the second overturned at a Paris street corner.

Steam, however, was not an immediate success on the roads, first because in those early days the roads themselves had surfaces so bad that we today can hardly imagine what they were like, and secondly because there were immense technical difficulties in scaling down the big steam engine to suit the small private carriage. Big steam carriages, which could carry sufficient coal, did have a vogue through the first part of the nineteenth century and indeed achieved a very fair measure of success especially on the continent. In England—with its Industrial Revolution and the momentous success of its network of railways—road traffic was deliberately squeezed out of existence. This was done by means of the Light Locomotives Act of 1865, now usually known as the 'Red Flag Act', which restricted speeds to four miles an hour in the country and two in town, and insisted on a man with a red flag walking in front of every automotive vehicle. This in itself probably amounted to a forty-year setback for England in the race to develop successful road vehicles.

It was the petrol engine that was to make the real story of the Motor Car. The steam engine was an *external* combustion engine—fire outside the engine produces the steam power to drive the pistons. How to release explosive power right inside the cylinders was the next problem to be faced and thus how to make an *internal combustion* engine. This began with the gas engine, the gas exploding within the engine, and was later developed with vaporized petrol—a story that belongs almost exclusively to Germany. I believe that the internal combustion engine has proved so important to the motor car that we must define the motor car by it. We do not call railway engines motor cars and in a very strict sense we should distinguish between motor cars and steam cars. The latter are decidedly not on the main road of motoring history. The early steam carriages, like the railway engine, contributed directly towards the development of the motor car and are therefore part of its history. This, in my opinion, is not true of the later steam cars of the Edwardian and Vintage periods. They seem to me to be running not on that main high-

Introduction

way of motoring history but on a little side road which merely happens to run parallel for some way before branching off into forgotten countryside.

Of course there were many other factors contributing to the development of the motor car. It is important to know these but it is equally important not to confuse them with the story of the car itself. High on this list is the amazing discovery of Macadam in the art of road making. Then there was the discovery of the explosive power of petrol. The story of the carriage through the ages, the story of the bicycle: these also form a very important part of the background story of the car. Look at the illustrations of the first light motor carriages and you will quickly see the influence of the old pennyfarthing bicycles turned into tuppence-farthing on the early three-wheelers and tuppence and two farthings on the 1898 Benz (Plate 1).

The young car historian will also want to ask more precise questions. He will want to know exactly the periods covered by the terms Veteran and Edwardian. He should know also the definition of the term Vintage so that he may avoid the popular confusion in the use of these terms. Lord Montagu, the founder of the famous Montagu Motor Museum, gives in his book, *The Motoring Montagus*, the proper definition of the different groups of 'Historic Cars'.

The definition of the Veteran car is one manufactured on or before 31st December 1904. These are the only cars that can enter the London to Brighton rally which takes place every November. They clatter along and some don't even manage the whole journey. This event used to be referred to as the 'Old Crocks Race', but today people are much more aware of the incredible pioneering leap forward from the horse, which they represent.

The Edwardian cars form the next group and some of these are really marvellous for their grace and elegance, for their gleaming brass acetylene lamps, for their bulb horns and for the variety of gadgets and instruments on their dashboards. These magnificent motor cars were made between 1st January 1905 and 31st December 1918, although the manufacture of private cars in Europe had ceased much earlier during the desperate battles of the First World War. During the Edwardian period, which has been stretched a little beyond the reign of King

Introduction

Edward VII to make more sensible grouping, cars tended to be made in small numbers and mainly belonged to the rich, though the idea of a popular car was starting to grow, especially in America where Henry Ford began the production of the ubiquitous Model T.

The Vintage era, which begins on 1st January 1919 and finishes on 31st December 1930, represents the popular fruition of all the pioneering work which is represented in this book.

These categories do make very sensible groupings and if you make the effort to remember them you will soon find that they start to give greater meaning to your museum visits. You will no longer be looking just at a gleaming mass of brass and paintwork and you will begin to grow familiar with the incredible story of the most revolutionary invention of all time.

2 · The Birth of the Motor Car in Germany

There is some doubt and a lot of argument about which really was the first motor car and it is indeed a very interesting question. There is no doubt, however, that the credit must go to Germany since all the vehicles which might merit this distinction were made by German engineers.

This great distinction is usually divided between Gottlieb Daimler and Carl Benz who both produced motor vehicles in the year 1885. They have generally become known as the fathers of the motor car but, in fact, a full ten years earlier Siegfried Marcus of Mecklenburg produced the motor car shown in the illustration below. Here was a motor car

2. The car made by Siegfried Marcus a decade before the cars of Daimler and Benz

with a four-stroke internal combustion engine, with four wheels and a steering wheel and with more of the authentic car look about it than many of the horseless carriages and flimsy three-wheelers which followed it. Even this was not Marcus's first car. As early as 1865 Marcus was

The Birth of the Motor Car in Germany

driving around in a cart powered by a two-stroke engine which was coupled directly to the rear wheels. It had no clutch and you had to hold the rear wheels off the ground while starting the engine.

The work of Marcus was forgotten, however, perhaps partly because he had so many other inventions and gadgets in which he was interested and partly because his vehicles were hounded off the road by people who were frightened of them and by the authorities. He was a man before his time. His work led to nothing and others were not ready to follow his lead. The work of Daimler and Benz, however, fits into a pattern of engineering development and it is very important to learn all about these men and their cars in order to understand the true foundations of motoring history.

One of the most important discoveries was that of the four-stroke engine made by Dr. N. A. Otto. Dr. Otto turned away from steam to develop an internal combustion engine which ran on coal gas. This became known as the 'Silent Gas Engine'. This engine works on what is now known as the Otto cycle: *induction*—drawing in the explosive gas when the piston is going down; *compression*—compressing it into the small space at the top of the cylinder as the piston is going up; *explosion*—exploding the compressed gas (or petrol vapour) which then of course drives the piston down, and finally *exhaust* which is when the piston as it comes up the next time forces the burnt gases out through the exhaust valve. Almost all cars now work on this system.

Gottlieb Daimler was an engineer at Dr. Otto's factory. He noticed that the oil companies, who were busily engaged upon producing vast quantities of paraffin for the improved oil lamps of the age, were also producing a waste product, which has since come to be called petrol! Daimler experimented with vaporizing this liquid through what has now come to be called a carburettor and using it to drive an engine, instead of gas, over which it had an obvious advantage. The gas engine could only operate on a site where there was a gas supply whereas the new petrol internal combustion engine could be mobile and fuel supplies were easily transportable. It was this that made the modern motor car possible.

Daimler, with his partner Wilhelm Maybach, left Dr. Otto's factory and started up his own experimental works. In 1885 he fitted a petrol

The Birth of the Motor Car in Germany

engine into a rather crude tricycle and in the following year made his first four-wheeled experimental car (Plate 2). His main interest was in developing his engine rather than the motor car as a whole. At that time a method known as hot tube ignition was used instead of sparking plugs to ignite the petrol. A device rather like a bunsen burner served to heat the tube which ignited the petrol. It was a crude method of ignition compared with the simple high tension spark used for the purpose today. The burner had to be lit every time you started up and the flame was liable to blow out as you drove along. What a performance, thinks the spoilt modern motorist! Whenever you are looking at the very early Veteran cars try to see for yourself the method of ignition used.

Carl Benz was the other great German who also fitted an engine into a three-wheeled vehicle in 1885 (Plate 3) and made his first four-wheeled motor car in 1886. These were exciting years though people at the time did not realize it. These contraptions, which they hardly knew whether to laugh at or be terrified of, were destined to change the world as surely as any political revolution or any war. You must strain your mind to realize that within a single lifetime the horse-drawn world, which had lasted for countless thousands of years, was abruptly transformed into the high-speed motorized world. Daimler and Benz were the two men, more than any others, who were responsible for this transformation. Benz produced a single-cylinder engine which was horizontally slung at the back of the carriage (Plate 4). It is an interesting engine because it is open, and worth examining closely. There is a splendid 1888 specimen in the Science Museum in London, which is carefully set in the centre of the

3. A clear illustration of the Tiller steering on the 1885 Benz, the type of steering used on the majority of cars before 1900

B 17

The Birth of the Motor Car in Germany

floor so that you can examine it all round. If you look from the back you can see right into the cylinder. You can see the connecting rod joining the piston to the completely exposed crankshaft. You can see the big flywheel underneath it. You had to spin this wheel to start the car. Note it does have an electrical sparking plug. You may also easily observe the belt drive system which transmits the power to the wheels. You may wonder how the engine worked with all the dust that must have been thrown on to it. It was crude and slow revving. Loose and wobbly bearings would not have had the same effect as they would on a modern high revving engine where fine tolerances are crucial. Benz's car was the first real practical car in the world. By 1901 he had sold over two thousand. His success, like that of Henry Ford on a much greater scale later, caused him to stick too long to his original design instead of seeking for radical improvements. The car which you can see for yourself in the Science Museum is the oldest petrol-driven car still existing in this country. The Museum catalogue describes it as 'the prototype of the world's automobile industry', and I think it true to regard Carl Benz as the father of the *automobile industry*. His thinking was in terms of a marketable product.

Daimler, on the other hand, should perhaps be regarded as the father of the *motor car engine*. Daimler was interested in developing through constant modification and experiment a successful relatively high revving engine. He encased his crankshaft, set his engine upright and achieved 900 revs per minute from it as opposed to the maximum 500 on the Benz engine. Daimler did not in fact think of cars as such. He thought of producing an engine which he could sell to people to fit into their own carriages and later on even turned much of his attention to suiting his engine to boats.

At this stage it is important to bear in mind the companies which developed from the work of these two great men. Remember that Daimler and Benz were entirely independent in the beginning and were even somewhat in competition. Sales of Benz cars began to be successful in Paris. Daimler sold his engines to other countries and also allowed them to be made under licence elsewhere, notably in France. His work under the direction of Wilhelm Maybach, after the influence of France had been reflected back on his company, was to lead to the creation of

The Birth of the Motor Car in Germany

one of the greatest cars of all time. A year after Daimler's death in 1900, Maybach produced the 1901 Mercedes (Plate 5). It had a modern style honeycomb radiator, a four-cylinder 35 h.p. engine, four-speed gearbox and a pressed steel chassis. It heralded the design and layout of the modern car. The century had turned and the motor car had grown away from the old horseless carriage. You may wonder why the Daimler had come to be called Mercedes. It was named after Mercedes Jellinek, the daughter of the Austro-Hungarian consul in Nice. The consul Emil Jellinek had given financial support to the sale and development of this highly successful model. Remember the Mercedes was a product of the Daimler company, not Benz. It was not until 1926 that the companies merged to form Mercedes-Benz as we know it today. It is quite important to get this little piece of history clear in your mind as the mixing up of these names can be very confusing.

Germany had made the first great effort that was to give birth to the motor car but neither Daimler nor Benz could have foreseen the explosive growth of their invention. It was in France that their products were chiefly sold and it was to that country that the manufacture and development of the motor car were rapidly to pass.

3 · *France—the Cradle of the Motor Car*

In 1889 Edouard Sarazin acted as an agent in forming one of the most important associations in motoring history. He brought Daimler into contact with the great French firm of Panhard et Levassor. Emile Levassor visited the Daimler works at Cannstatt with the result that his firm obtained the concession to manufacture Daimler engines in France.

In order to understand the full significance of this we have to look back at some of the important developments of the steam road vehicle which had taken place in France during the years when Marcus, Daimler and Benz were working on their petrol-driven cars in Austria and Germany. Several very famous motoring pioneers were at work: Amédée Bollée, Count Albert de Dion and Léon Serpollet. Bollée produced a

4. 'L'Obéissante', the steam omnibus built by Bollée in 1873 with independent front suspension and individually pivoted wheels

France—the Cradle of the Motor Car

large steam carriage of the old heavy type which carried quantities of coal to produce steam, but it was a remarkably well-constructed vehicle and had two very important features which are now used on the modern motor car: independent front suspension and front wheels which pivoted on separate stub axles. Before that time the whole front axle had pivoted at the centre as had been the case for centuries on horse-drawn carriages. It is important to try to get a clear picture in your mind of what this change means. Think of how well the old centrally pivoted axle was suited to the harnessing of the horse. Think also how impossible it would be to build a modern motor car if the whole front axle had to swivel! Daimler built his first car in this way and very unsatisfactory it was. De Dion saw the difficulty of carrying solid fuel around on a small road vehicle and developed the idea of using petrol or paraffin to heat the boiler. He made a small practical steam road vehicle in 1887. One of the greatest developments in the use of steam power was made by Léon Serpollet. The old method had been by a boiler which took some time to heat up. Serpollet realized that if water could be poured into a red-hot tube steam could be produced immediately. Perhaps you have at sometime or other poured a little water on red-hot metal and noticed how it is turned instantaneously into sizzling steam. Thus the 'flash' type steam car was added to the boiler-driven vehicle.

These were indeed very interesting developments. In addition to these obviously new developments very many old ideas had been refined but no one in France, or indeed anywhere else in the world, had concentrated like Daimler on the internal combustion petrol engine. As soon as Emile Levassor saw Daimler's engine he realized that here was the engine for the ideal car he was then dreaming up. This led to the creation of the *Système Panhard et Levassor* (often just referred to as the Système Panhard). The final layout of the modern car had been achieved. Levassor put Daimler's engine in between the front wheels, thereby putting much more weight on them and immensely improving the steering qualities of his car. He covered the engine with a bonnet. He used a modern friction type clutch to disengage the drive of the engine from the wheels. He set a gearbox behind the engine and the drive to the rear wheels was through a chain. Although this new layout of Levassor's

France—the Cradle of the Motor Car

did not include a single original item, his car became one of the great landmarks in motoring history and Maybach was to get good returns for Daimler's wonderful engine when he came to make the 1901 Mercedes which was, of course, built on the Système Panhard et Levassor. The Panhard is another car you should try to look at closely. There is a good example of this car in the Science Museum (Plate 6). Notice the two little brass doors on the front. They are usually left open so that you can see a good example of hot-tube ignition. Petrol flames are used to heat the platinum tubes.

Although John Boyd Dunlop had already made the pneumatic tyre for the bicycle and had had considerable success with it during the Victorian cycling craze, he had no faith in it for use on heavy vehicles. The production of the first successful(?) air-filled tyres occurred in France in 1895 when the Michelin brothers fitted a Peugeot with a set of pneumatic tyres. The car was entered for the Paris to Bordeaux race of that year and although it had to drop out after no less than twenty-two new inner tubes had been fitted, the taste of the bliss of riding on air which the Michelin brothers experienced was enough to make them persevere towards the world wide fame their firm possesses today.

The name of Renault is still very prominent on the motoring scene throughout the world. It is quite comic to see Louis Renault, the founder of the Renault concern, sitting on his absurdly small car and looking rather like Charlie Chaplin in one of his silent films. His odd little car contained a feature which was soon to become universal in car manufacture. For the first time a car was fitted with a sprung rear axle with a differential driven by a propeller shaft from the gear-box. It is worth pausing for a moment and thinking about this 'live' rear axle, as it is called. We now take this aspect of transmission for granted, but it was really revolutionary in its day. What, you may ask, was so revolutionary about it? To understand the answer to this question you need to know why until that time the final drive from the engine was usually transmitted by a chain and sprockets. The reason is simple. The chain could take the strain of the whole weight and momentum of the car. To put all that strain directly on a few small teeth of the crown wheel and pinion in the back axle was asking quite a lot because the strain is concentrated on to tiny pieces of metal. There is no cushioning or tensioning in the

France—the Cradle of the Motor Car

5. Louis Renault sitting up at the wheel of his first voiturette, his first car

drive. That, of course, is why it is called 'live'. Heavier cars had to continue using chain drive for some time until strong enough metals could be developed for them also to be fitted for 'live' rear axles, which was something that was to be achieved for the first time by a great British car.

The cars produced by Count Albert de Dion and Georges Bouton are among the most famous and well known of Veteran cars. Most of us have seen the film *Genevieve* and remember the de Dion Boutons which were seen in that excellent veteran car comedy. There is another splendid de Dion Bouton in the Montagu Motor Museum, the original car of the Museum, having been in the Montagu family since 1913. It is a 6 h.p. model-Q of 1903 and has the single-cylinder engine for which the company is famed. It was one of these engines that powered Louis Renault's first car.

At this point you may well be wondering why France took over the

France—the Cradle of the Motor Car

6. 1903 de Dion Bouton

lead from Germany. France was probably the only country in the world which could have developed the motor car. She was the only country that had the roads to do so. The long, straight, paved roads built by Napoleon to facilitate the rapid movement of his armies now played a key role in allowing the motor car to develop. France was free of motoring restrictions because she did have roads on which cars could be driven and even raced. We often forget that the cars of today only run as well as they do because of the magnificent glass-smooth surfaces which are provided for them. Most would fall to pieces if they were driven over the pot-holed dirt tracks which were the roads of the 1890s. It was the roads of France that caused Frenchmen to buy the original German invention and without the French market the motor car might well have fizzled out.

The story of the great early motor races began in 1894 with the race from Paris to Rouen. All types of cars entered and the race was actually won by a de Dion Bouton steam car. Another race—this time from Paris to Bordeaux and back—took place the following year. It was won by a Panhard driven by Emile Levassor himself. He averaged nearly 15 m.p.h. for over 700 miles and put up a personal record which has never been beaten in the history of motoring: 48 hours and 47 minutes of continuous unaided driving! Here indeed was the first proof of the superiority of his 'système'. This was quickly noticed by Daimler who adopted that

France—the Cradle of the Motor Car

layout for his own cars. If you look at Daimlers after this time you will be able to see it clearly for yourself. One year later still, in 1896, an even more ambitious race was organized: Paris to Marseilles and back, a distance of over 1,000 miles. This time Levassor hit a large dog between Avignon and Orange and overturned his car. He finished the race but died mysteriously the following year, probably due to some internal injury suffered in the accident.

These races, as you can see from pictures of the cars taking part, were for cars manufactured for ordinary use on the roads. After 1900 a new phase in racing was to develop. Monster racing cars began to be built specially for the purpose. Fabulous they were too, terrifyingly dangerous and dramatic. But that is a separate story. Now we must return to England.

4 · The Handicapped Beginnings of British Motoring

What, during all this time, was happening in England? The British Empire was at its zenith under Queen Victoria and England was the leading industrial power of the world. Yet she was neither making nor developing motor cars. Only a knowledge of history can explain this amazing paradox. It was precisely because of our early industrial development that we had created before any other country a vast network of railways and an extensive system of canal waterways. These carried both our passengers and our heavy goods and we had no pressing need for good roads. The railways had a transport monopoly and they certainly did not wish to lose it. They saw motor cars as something that would steal their business. Many men in power in the government had invested heavily in the railways and they did not wish to see any competition arise which might take their profits away. Maybe also a few had the foresight to sense the impossible situations which vast numbers of individually driven vehicles would bring to our towns and cities and so opposed the motor car from disinterested motives. Opposition was first directed against the potential successes of the early steam coaches and in good time a blow was dealt against all road vehicles by the Light Locomotives Act of 1865. They were restricted to the ludicrous speeds of 4 m.p.h. in the country and 2 m.p.h. in the towns. To add final insult to an already sufficiently injurious act it was ordered that a man with a red flag was to walk in front of every self-propelled road vehicle! What chance had the motor car got in England?

There were, however, other strong forces at work. Certain rich and powerful men went to see for themselves what was happening on the Continent of Europe. They perhaps envied and certainly wished to emulate the brilliant motoring successes of France. These men with Sir David Salomons as their leader formed the Self-propelled Traffic Association. They organized the first 'motor display' at Tunbridge Wells in 1895 and held the very first Motor Show in London in the following

The Handicapped Beginnings of British Motoring

year. In the same year the 'Red Flag Act', as it had come to be called, was repealed and the first London to Brighton Run was staged to commemorate the association's success (Plate 7). And it has gone on ever since annually without interruption except during time of war. Although the way to motoring in England had at last been opened up, all the cars which took part in the event were Continental.

Cars had been made in England before 1896 but they had been consigned to oblivion. They, like the cars of Siegfried Marcus, had arrived before their time. The products of Edward Butler and J. H. Knight played little part in the history of motor development but they are an interesting part of our own country's motoring heritage. Butler built the motorized tricycle shown in Plate 8 as early as 1887. Its close affinity to the bicycle is unmistakable. J. H. Knight of Farnham built the much more substantial vehicle shown below in 1895. It can still be seen in the Montagu Motor Museum. A word of warning must be given here. In its original version it was built with only one front

7. John Henry Knight driving the car he made in 1895, which can still be seen in the Montagu Motor Museum

The Handicapped Beginnings of British Motoring

wheel. The extra wheel was added later as a modification carried out by Knight himself. When you hear Frederick Lanchester mentioned as the first builder of a four-wheeled car do not make the mistake of thinking you have found an earlier four-wheeler. Don't try to find the historians wrong where early cars are concerned. Much better to be always on the look-out for tell-tale signs of later modification. Always bear in mind that these early cars were the productions of an extremely experimental stage in motoring history. Later alterations were frequent on 'one off' cars. Look for them but don't be deceived by them.

It is necessary also not to be deceived by the names of this early Veteran period. Anthony Bird in his *Profile* on the Wolseley puts the matter very bluntly, 'On paper a thriving British motor industry existed before 1900. . . . Many of the importations were disguised with English names and a number of English firms started making English copies of Continental designs. The Triumph for example was really a Renault. The Star was a Wolverhampton copy of a Benz.'

From 1900 we may begin to look for the real beginnings of the British motor industry, existing and competing in its own right. Three important events stimulated this development. First there was the already mentioned repeal of the Red Flag Act. Secondly the seal of royal approval was accorded to motoring when the present Lord Montagu's father took King Edward VII (then Prince of Wales) for a ride in his Daimler (Plate 9). Thirdly the Automobile Club, which has since become the R.A.C. and which was founded in 1897, organized the famous 1,000 mile round Britain trial. Nearly half the cars completed the run which was won by the Hon. C. S. Rolls driving a 12 h.p. Panhard-Levassor. He made only one involuntary stop during the whole journey. This event did a great deal to convince the British public of the practicability of motoring. Three great new British names appeared on the list of entries: Lanchester, Napier and Wolseley. The last two still owed much to continental firms but they were soon to shake themselves free of this and become very great names in their own right (Plate 10).

Before embarking on a short survey of British cars of the early part of the century it is a good idea to try to understand some of the general trends in car body design. If you do not get these clear in your mind you are liable to get a very mixed-up picture of car development. If you do

The Handicapped Beginnings of British Motoring

try to follow the trends you will find you have discovered a source of constantly revealing clues to the confusing mass of machinery produced in the motor car world.

In the first place most cars were of the open variety. People were far too concerned with merely making them work to be bothered with boxing them in or adding any of the other refinements which we now take for granted. Some firms like Daimler had tried to fix their engines to carriages. Others had arranged for the old and famous coach makers to fit bodies to their larger chasses. These generally became known as town cars or carriages. They were genuinely in the horseless carriage tradition and were probably rightly considered not to be fit to face the rough country roads where the speed limit had been increased to 20 m.p.h. A little later there developed a medium range of car, medium powered and soon acquiring the half protection of a hood and windscreen. These became known as *tourers* for the very simple reason that they could be driven on tours out of town without too high an expectation of the body falling

8. 7 h.p. Alldays and Onions car of 1904—a very typical car of the period

to pieces. The term tourer is still used today to describe an open car with a hood that folds down in spite of the fact that now millions more

The Handicapped Beginnings of British Motoring

saloon cars go touring than tourers! At the end of the scale came the *voiturettes*—the French term for their little cars. These, as you can see from many of the illustrations, were much more in the nature of motorized tricycles or quadricycles than horseless carriages. And it is very interesting to note how many famous bicycle manufacturers turned to car manufacturing, Rover and Humber being just two examples. The economy of producing bicycle parts which could be adapted to motorized contraptions contributed to the cheaper production of early small cars. A few models lie awkwardly between these categories but they will help you to see your way towards the fairly settled types of car which had arrived by the end of the Edwardian period.

The large car which dominated the scene at the beginning of the century was the great Mercedes of 1901. It outclassed everything else on the racing circuit and set the style for the monster racing cars of the first decade of the century. The first serious opposition to the success of the Mercedes came from England in the form of the great six-cylinder Napier. It had the distinction of being the first large car to have a 'live' rear axle. This was remarkable at this early stage since many racing cars were chain-driven right into the Vintage period. A Napier won the Gordon Bennett Trophy in 1902 and Montague Napier made use of the racing successes of the marque to develop his domestic market.

Although the Napier proved a great success with wealthy sporting types, it was not the sort of car to recommend itself to the more sedate members of the British aristocracy who were accustomed to the quiet comfort of the old horse carriage. The Napier was neither smooth nor silent. The fulfilment of the dreams of the most fastidious dowager duchess was to be found in the immortal Rolls-Royce Silver Ghost of 1907 (Plate 11). There is, of course, a great story behind the creation of that legendary car. The Hon. Charles S. Rolls, already mentioned in this chapter as the winner of the 1,000 Miles Trial in fine sporting fashion, had had a succession of the latest Panhards and had been dashing across to the Continent to participate in the great French races, while in London he had organized a motor agency with Claude Johnson to sell Panhard-Levassor cars in England. At the same time and unknown to him Frederick Henry Royce was travelling around in his second-hand French Decauville and had founded the small firm of Royce Limited.

The Handicapped Beginnings of British Motoring

He had begun by producing electrical components but disgust with the quality and workmanship of his own small secondhand French car made him turn to the building of a car himself, which would come up to the standards that he himself expected. The prototypes of the 10 h.p. car appeared in 1904. The meeting of Rolls and Royce is briefly described by George Oliver in his *Profile* on the 15 h.p. Rolls-Royce: 'What ensued is well enough known by now; Rolls, a motorist of great experience and at the time head of the firm C. S. Rolls & Co., Motor Agents, was persuaded to travel to Manchester to Royce and to try his little car, was delighted by the quality of its construction and the manner of its going, and, with the enthusiastic support of his fellow director, the great Claude Johnson, entered soon after into an agreement with Royce Limited for the exclusive supply of a whole range of cars.' These included a two-cylinder 10 h.p. car, a three-cylinder 15 h.p. car, a four-cylinder 20 h.p. car and a six-cylinder 30 h.p. car. The first interesting little catalogue of 1905 produced by C. S. Rolls and Co. reflects, perhaps a little naively, the motoring situation of the times; it says that in response to 'the constant pressure brought to bear upon them to produce in this country a motor vehicle of the VERY HIGHEST GRADE, which will compare favourably with the best Continental makes, they have after much experiment perfected and placed on the market AN ALL-BRITISH CAR' (that phrase is in large red letters!). All this led to the incomparable Silver Ghost of 1906/7, the car that became known as the finest car in the world. It was bought by kings, princes and statesmen everywhere. It was used as an armoured car in the First World War, and Lenin had one to drive around in when he was reorganizing Russia after the Revolution. The practical effect of the way in which this wonderful car was made was that bits and pieces didn't break or work loose on a Rolls as they did on other cars. Every part was subjected to rigorous testing not only in prototype form as happens with production models today but in the case of every single car Rolls-Royce produced. Each car was made, driven and dismantled down to the smallest item and then carefully checked and reassembled before being delivered to its buyer. Try to have a close look at a Silver Ghost. Both the Montagu Motor Museum and the Science Museum have one. Look at the magnificent 40/50 h.p. side-valve engine with its capacity of

The Handicapped Beginnings of British Motoring

7,046 c.c.! Note how the top of the engine is divided into two blocks with three pistons operating in each block. When you look closely at the mechanism of the Rolls-Royce I am sure you will be amazed by the vast number of closely spaced nuts and bolts which hold all the parts together. Nothing was left to chance. A special system of dual ignition was used. Each cylinder was served by two sparking plugs, one working from a magneto, a special device for producing *high-tension* sparks, the other working from a coil which transformed the *low-tension* current from the battery. By this dual system one of the most common causes of breakdown on the road, ignition failure, was almost eliminated. Royce, like Levassor in France, did not invent anything new. His genius lay in selecting the very best of everything that was available at the time for his car which he then constructed in the most painstaking manner so as almost to eliminate the chance of breakdown. One ran faultlessly for the 15,000 mile R.A.C. observed trial of 1907 and the model was so successful in the even more important reliability trials of life that it continued to be made until 1925.

It was natural that in those early pioneering days stories tended to revolve round great personalities. At the turn of the century Herbert Austin was chief designer at the Wolseley Sheep Shearing Machine Company. The fortunes of the company were low and Austin hoped to restore them by turning to motor manufacture. He began by designing a little tricar in 1896 and went on to produce tourers of increasing size: 3 h.p., then 6 h.p., going on up to the 20 and 24 h.p. tourers which fall within the category of medium-sized touring cars. They were all fitted with horizontally opposed engines. They were noisy and not very beautiful, but they were extremely reliable for their time. Reports of their remarkable endurance began to trickle in from the outposts of the British Empire, from Malaya, India, Africa and Australia. Austin had a brain that was always bubbling over with new ideas and he was involved in everything (Plate 12). He made racing cars for Wolseley which he took across for events in France and he turned to making his own cars in 1905. He brought out a 25/30 h.p. tourer in 1906 and followed it by as wide a variety of models as ever any firm produced. The famous Baby Austin Seven came after the Edwardian period, but a design borrowed from the Swift motor company was used for the 1909 single-

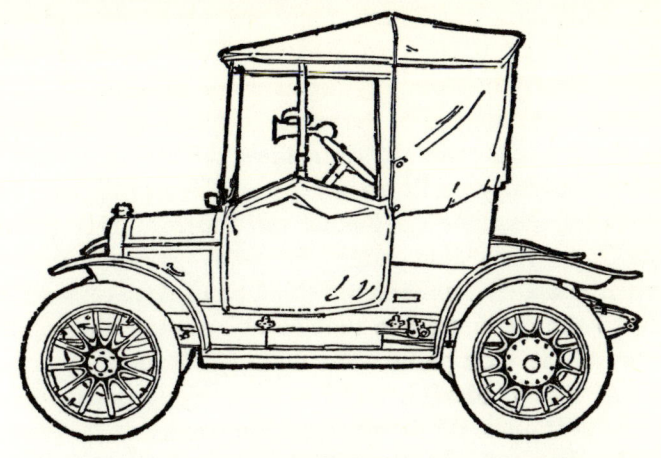

The Handicapped Beginnings of British Motoring

9. Swift-designed single-cylinder Austin 7 which came out in 1909

cylinder Austin Seven, an example of which can be seen in the Montagu Motor Museum. Austin was also busy at the other end of the scale as you can see from the giant racer in Plate 22.

This 1907 16/20 h.p. Sunbeam is another example of the medium-powered British touring car of the mid-Edwardian period. The bonnet is

10. 1907 16/20 h.p. Sunbeam—a typical example of a good medium-range car of the period

The Handicapped Beginnings of British Motoring

low but the bodywork is still high; there are side doors, and a windscreen and hood have become standard features. Such cars were fulfilling the needs of the slightly less wealthy members of society.

Right at the opposite end of the scale from the very expensive Napiers and Rolls-Royces of the wealthy came the small cars or voiturettes. These stemmed from an early tradition in France. Remember the voiturette of Louis Renault. In England the first cars of Butler and Knight were really in this tradition. They were indeed far away from the great horseless carriages of the rich. To understand this line of development we have to look back to the cycling craze that spread across Victorian England: the Humber Cycle Company were making bicycles, Rover produced their famous 'safety' bicycle. Bicycles were being mass-produced. For that reason the frames, the wheels and the parts generally were obtainable cheaply. A couple of bicycles fixed side by side and a motor of some sort to power the contraption and there was the poor man's car. Some, of course, only had three wheels but the best firms began to develop stout little voiturettes. Humber brought out their first car in 1902, Rover in 1904 (Plate 13). It is interesting to note the backyard atmosphere in which some of the greatest names in the motor industry

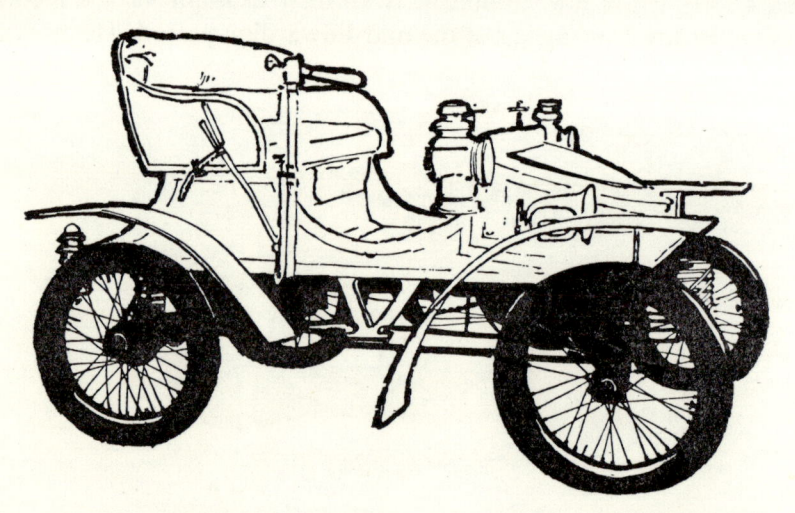

11. One of Vauxhall's first cars made in 1903/4. Note the typical bonnet shape of the marque

The Handicapped Beginnings of British Motoring

had their origins. In 1903 Vauxhall, an entirely new firm, made their first car with tiller steering, 5 h.p. single-cylinder horizontally mounted engine, just two forward gears, no reverse and a price of only £150. A new attitude to motoring was growing up and a letter from a certain Dr. Home about this new small Vauxhall shows clearly the way in which people were beginning to think:

'The wear and tear driving at 15 m.p.h. is, in my opinion, almost of negligible quantity. The average cost of running (daily) has worked out one-third that of the upkeep of my horse. . . . I have at present never experienced a moment's worry on the road. . . . An inexpensive, reliable and comfortable means of locomotion, say I.' (*The Autocar*, 1904.)

Already money was settling the future of the motor car. The Automobile Association started up at the beginning of the century. A great part of its purpose was to warn motorists of traps set by police forces still traditionally hostile to motoring. Cars first had to be registered in 1904 and number-plates carried, thus making even easier the job of prejudiced police. Despite our belated and handicapped start in the motoring field, when we did get going motor manufacturers sprang up in greater profusion than anywhere else in Europe. It is hard to make

12. 1906 6 h.p. Calthorpe

The Handicapped Beginnings of British Motoring

your way through the multitude of names but I shall make a haphazard list of the better-known names. See if you can fit them into the scheme I've suggested. The 1906 Calthorpe, with its strange high hood, its wire wheels and 6 h.p. single-cylinder engine, is not hard to place. Standard produced their first car, with a 6 h.p. single-cylinder engine, three-speed gear-box and shaft drive, in 1903 (Plate 14). A.C. produced some commercial three-wheelers known as Auto Carriers, from which humble origin this very fine make derived its name (Plate 15). In 1909 they pro-

13. The A.C. Sociable which appeared in 1909

duced their Sociable, a little three-wheeled passenger vehicle with a $5\frac{1}{2}$ h.p. engine. This was sold at £90, but it is interesting to note that the hood was six guineas extra if you wanted it. Windscreen, sidelamps and bulb horn were also optional extras. The Siddeley Autocar Company was also in operation and merged with Wolseley to produce the Wolseley-Siddeley when Herbert Austin left the company to set up on his own. The prototype of the small Jowett appeared in 1906. Lea Francis made their 15/20 h.p. car in 1903. Lagonda, a name associated with splendid luxury sports cars of the 'twenties, were making motor cycles and tricars from 1898 onwards. An interesting point to look for on the 1906 ex-

The Handicapped Beginnings of British Motoring

ample in the Montagu Motor Museum is the braking system which is applied to all the wheels, contrary to the standard practice of the time. Even Henry Royce didn't fit brakes on the front wheels of his cars. In fact he did not do so for a very long time because he believed it interfered with the quality of the steering. Another very great three-wheeler came out in 1909. H. F. S. Morgan built a three-wheeled car for himself in his own garage at Malvern (Plate 16). Into it he fitted a 7 h.p. twin-cylinder air-cooled J.A.P. engine. It was the beginning of a line of really great three-wheelers and the four-wheeled sports cars which are still made today on an individual, hand-made basis. Three other great makes came into car production from cycle making: Sunbeam, Triumph and Star. There were many other odd names about, but it is important to get to know the really famous makes first and to know them thoroughly. Lanchester, Napier, Rolls-Royce, Wolseley, Austin and Morris, these cars and the men associated with them form the foundations of your knowledge of Veteran and Edwardian cars in England.

5 · *The Edwardian Era on the Continent*

France not only led the way in motoring in the very early days but also managed to retain an impressive leading position in styling and mechanical design during the Edwardian period. It is really important to know something about the leading French makes in detail. You have already heard of the sporting young Charles Rolls hurrying across to France with his latest Panhards which he considered the best and most reliable cars in the world until he became acquainted with the cars of Henry Royce. Panhard continued to make a variety of models using their well-

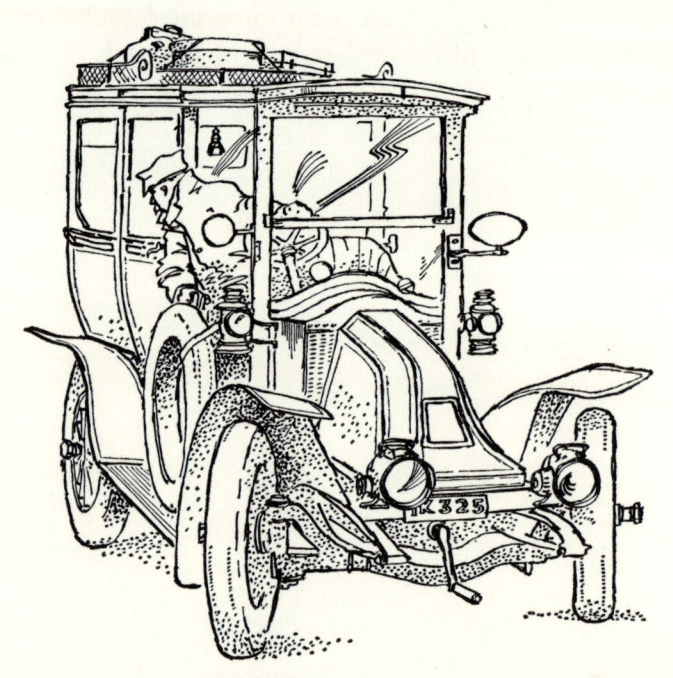

14. 1906 Renault 20/30 h.p. car with typical 'coal shovel' bonnet and interior design like a 1st class railway carriage of the period

The Edwardian Era on the Continent

proven 'Système'. The Renault brothers continued also to develop their cars from the first little voiturette of Louis Renault. They used de Dion Bouton engines until 1902 when they started making their own. Soon the very distinctive Renault bonnet shape appeared. They produced cars in the whole range of sizes: from little two-cylinder tourers to the great six-cylinder 35 CV of 1912. Their cars were widely used as taxis and it was in these that an historic movement of troops to the Marne was carried out in March 1914 in preparation for the First World War. You can always recognize a Vintage Renault by the characteristic diamond-shaped badge with 'RENAULT' written across it in clear capital letters. In Veteran and Edwardian days the badge was round. Peugeot, another great concern that has persisted successfully since the earliest days, you should also know. Like many firms in England Peugeot had manufactured bicycles and in fact had existed as a firm since the days of the French Revolution. They are known for their small cars,

15. The Bébé Peugeot of 1912 with 850 c.c. engine and structurally the forerunner of the baby Austins and Morrises of the Vintage period

especially the 1912 Bébé. It was designed by Ettore Bugatti and was the 'original' baby car, the forerunner of the Baby Austins and Morris Minors of the Vintage period.

Bollée, Darracq, Delage, Delahaye, Mors and Gobron-Brillié are the

The Edwardian Era on the Continent

major names associated with early French racing. The last of these, the Gobron-Brillié, had a remarkable engine of the vertical, opposed-piston type, with two pistons per cylinder! It was very efficient and enabled Gobron-Brillié to set the land speed record several times in 1903 and 1904.

The little Decauville made by a locomotive works at the beginning of the century will always be remembered by the fact that it inspired and disgusted Henry Royce into building the finest and most expensive cars in the world. At the other end of the scale came the French counterpart of Rolls-Royce, the Delaunay-Belleville. Like the Dutch Spyker with which most of us are familiar through the film *Genevieve*, many of its models had round radiators as in the illustration below. It also was sought after by kings and princes.

16. The grand 27 h.p. Delaunay of 1911

The development of the racing car as such will be considered more fully in a later chapter but one aspect of racing is important here. The belief grew up that power is increased by the increase in the size of the

The Edwardian Era on the Continent

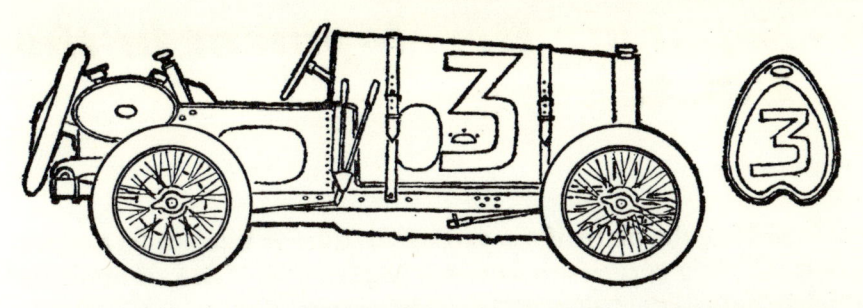

17. Racing version of the Bugatti Type 13, the Brescia, with frontal view of radiator, inset

engine. This view was challenged in practice by one of the greatest of all designers, Ettore Bugatti. It was probably no accident that the economic mind of the man who designed the Bébé Peugeot should have produced his own small car, the Type 13 Bugatti. Most designers, because of the limitations of metallurgy and other factors, stuck to the safety of side-valve engines. Bugatti changed this. L. T. C. Rolt writes of this in his *Motoring History*:

'The most daring and successful exception to this rule was Ettore Bugatti, who, in 1910, designed a car which was as important a milestone in motoring history as the Panhard or the 1901 Mercedes. This little Type 13 Bugatti had an engine of only 1,327 c.c., but it had overhead valves, driven by an overhead camshaft, and it revved up with the smoothness and alacrity of a turbine to 3,000 r.p.m. This gave the car a mile a minute performance, as it proved in 1911 when it finished second to a giant F.I.A.T. of $10\frac{1}{2}$ litres capacity.... By proving that there was a way of obtaining speed without multiplying litres, Ettore Bugatti sounded the death knell of the "giant racer".'

Technical development also continued in Germany but a great deal of the work was a reflection of French technical advance. Names such as Opel, Adler and NSU came on to the scene. Daimler improved their Mercedes, and Benz, after hanging on to the original limited design for too long, produced the *Blitzen-Benz* which set the world record for 1909 at 125·95 m.p.h. With Mercedes this set a new trend of absolute technical excellence which was always to keep Germany in the lead in racing whenever she was participating.

6 · *Separate Development in the U.S.A.*

If the car took the place of the carriage in Europe it might be said that it took the place of the farm or ranch buggy in the U.S.A. It developed on fairly independent lines and only in respect of mass production—a process which had already begun with many other products—was the American motor car industry ahead of Europe in the Veteran period. Technically and in respect of style it was far behind Europe. The first American car, made by Charles and Frank Duryea in 1893, was a crude affair as is plain from the illustration below. If you happen to be in America you can see the original specimen in the National Museum in Washington.

Three years later another one of the very greatest characters in motor-

18. 1893 Duryea, the first American motor car

Separate Development in the U.S.A.

ing history, Henry Ford, made his first car (Plate 17). It was a homemade affair which Ford constructed in a shed in the garden after he had finished his day's work as an electrical engineer. As you can see from the illustration Ford, like Benz, followed the bicycle tradition. The engine was set at the back and the final drive to one of the rear wheels was by sprocket and chain. Various models—A, B, C, D and so on—followed (Plate 18). These days it is often thought that Ford was simply the producer of a cheap car. 'If you can't afford a car you can a Ford,' people jeered. A little of the Ford story will help you to avoid this error. In 1902 Ford built his own racing car and challenged Alexander Winton, the track champion of the United States, whom he beat in spite of the fact that he had never driven in a race before. He went on to build his even more famous racer, the 999. It was in the twin of this car that in 1904 Ford himself took the world speed record at 91·37 m.p.h. Henry Ford was certainly interested in big, expensive, fine cars and he was a dedicated engineer before he was a salesman. After his successes, which brought him to the notice of all America, he turned his energies to mass production, to the idea of giving (or almost giving) everybody a motor car, and with that wonderful publicity behind him he set about producing the greatest all-round car of all time, 'the Universal Car' as he himself called the Model T Ford. This is a car that you should certainly get to know inside out, and you will find that you can make fascinating comparisons with other cars and find out how many great designers followed Ford's ideas. The Model T was first made in 1908 and remained in production until 1927, by which time over 15,000,000 had been made. From 1910 onwards the Model T was also made at the Trafford Park factory in Manchester. Right at the end of the Edwardian period 40 per cent of *all* motor vehicles registered in England were Fords! Why was the Model T so successful? Ford decided to make his popular car good, solid, reliable and cheap. You may have heard people talk of Tin Lizzies but, in fact, Ford's cars were made of the finest materials and every part was ruggedly built. You can still see them running about on the farms in the Mid West corn-belt and on the great estancias (cattle farms) of Argentina, where today they fetch seven or eight times their original price, not to be put into museums but to travel daily over bumpy farm tracks. If you crawl underneath you will

Separate Development in the U.S.A.

19. Model T Ford of 1909

see that the layout of the chassis and front suspension has marked similarities to that of the later Austin Seven. Many small continental cars also followed this pattern and used transverse front suspension. Model Ts also had their idiosyncrasies which practically nobody followed. Look at the four trembler coils under the scuttle, which serve the four plugs with electricity produced by a generator built into the flywheel of the engine. To us today the Model T may seem a little odd to drive: the left-hand pedal operates the two forward speeds and the centre pedal works reverse, through a system of gearing known as epicyclic. The right-hand pedal operates the transmission brake. The car's 2·9 litre engine took it up to about 40 m.p.h. maximum and its high ground clearance made it most valuable in wild, open, cowboy country of the United States. At that time when tracks were the only roads no one asked for a greater performance than the Model T offered. With this car the man who had said that history was bunk had shown how he could change it. He transformed the motoring scene and 'inspired' or 'drove' every would-be mass producer in the world to efforts which otherwise might never have been dreamed of. It is probably no exaggera-

Separate Development in the U.S.A.

tion to say that the whole history of the modern mechanized world might have been held back a hundred years without Henry Ford.

If, as was clearly the case, the Ford Motor Company was the undisputed product of an individual, the other great car manufacturer of the United States, General Motors, was an anonymous concern which contrived to suck in a mass of great individual engineers and firms so that apart from Ford most of America's automobile pioneers, not to mention certain great British and European firms, ended up within its confines. Ransom Eli Olds made the first really popular American car, the 'Curved Dash' Oldsmobile of 1901. The standardization of its parts

20. The 'Curved Dash' Oldsmobile, the first popular American car which came into production in 1901

and the mass production methods used to produce it account for its wide sales, but the car from the engineering point of view was far behind what was then being made in Europe. The Système Panhard-Levassor had not then been introduced and the 'Curved Dash' with its engine at the rear was still very similar to the even then old-fashioned Benz of fifteen years earlier. Still it was something of a jolly make in America and its promoters played on this when they put out their next model with the song 'In my merry Oldsmobile'.

Cadillac, who also found their way into General Motors, produced

Separate Development in the U.S.A.

an excellent little enclosed carriage around 1904. In 1908 they won the British Dewar Trophy for an almost incredible demonstration of the standardization of the parts. Three cars were totally dismantled. The parts then were completely mixed up in a great heap. Three fresh cars were built from the bits and immediately driven. That was something that could never have been done with European cars at that time. Variations and alterations were constantly being made and every individual car was subject to modification. Cadillac won the Dewar Trophy again in 1913 for its electric starter. These were two very important events. The demonstration of standardization of parts must have had a very profound effect on men such as Austin and Morris who were on the verge of starting mass production in England. Other great names which came within the G.M. organization are Buick, Chevrolet, Oakland. All produced early cars during the Veteran and Edwardian periods. Many chapters could be written on the early history of cars in America. I have tried to pick out the features which affected international car development. Perhaps the oddity known as the Pennington Autocar, a three-wheeler made by E. J. Pennington in 1896, ought to be mentioned in this context. Pennington claimed he had found all the final answers to motor car design. His claims were fantastic, as we can now see, but in his day he influenced Henry Ford and persuaded the Humber Company to build his strange vehicle, the only known survivor being in the Montagu Motor Museum. It is worth having a look at it to see how many of his ideas were ultimately not used.

In the sporting field America also had its great successes. Henry Ford, as already mentioned, participated actively with his cars. Great European drivers and cars usually proved their superiority in America's annual racing event for the Vanderbilt Cup, until it was won by a great American racer, the Locomobile, in 1908. The Mercer 35J Raceabout, a true sports car, shows America's progress in this specialist field by 1913. Again it is not possible here to trace the story of American sports and racing cars. We must cross the Atlantic again to learn about the Mecca of all motoring adventure and experimentation.

7 · Brooklands and the Dawn of Motor Racing

The French races of the 1890s were really endurance tests for ordinary production cars. They paved the way to fantastically rapid technical progress. The Paris to Madrid race of 1903, on the other hand, was in every sense a race. Monster racing cars had been specially built for the purpose and speeds of up to 90 m.p.h. were achieved on ordinary roads. Racers were killed—Louis Renault heard of the death of his brother Marcel just as he was celebrating his own triumph in Bordeaux —spectators including children were killed, and the race was stopped by the French Government. The newspapers described it as 'the Race to Death'. The cars were towed by horses to the station at Bordeaux and returned to Paris by train. The great French racing ace Gabriel driving a 70 h.p. Mors was declared the winner. He *averaged* 65·3 m.p.h. for the 342 miles from Paris to Bordeaux. When one recalls the strict speed limits enforced in towns this is quite astonishing and means that some of the cars must have been travelling at 90 m.p.h. along narrow roads on which the odd old farmer might at any moment emerge on his horse and cart! Louis Renault's performance was even more amazing. He achieved an average of 62·3 m.p.h. on his own 30 h.p. car—'a statement which fills one with awe as one writes it,' says Laurence Pomeroy in his book *The Evolution of the Racing Car*. Great as these results were, the public outcry against the tragedy of the event was so great that it spelt the end of racing on the open road.

The Gordon Bennett Trophy race of July 1903 was the first to be held on a circuit of closed roads. In the previous year the British entry included Herbert Austin himself driving a Wolseley and S. F. Edge in a Napier, and it turned out to be a remarkable triumph for Britain. The back axle of the leading Panhard broke only thirty miles from the finishing line and Edge drove in with his Napier. 'That a British car should beat the cream of the French motor industry was a sensation,' writes Laurence Pomeroy, but it was also an embarrassment since

Brooklands and the Dawn of Motor Racing

according to the terms of the trophy the winning entry has the honour of organizing the following year's race and it would need an Act of Parliament to run it in England. The problem was solved by holding it in the south of Ireland which was then still part of the United Kingdom. The feelings of all enthusiastic motorists in England must have been deeply wounded by what should have been a great honour.

In 1904 another memorable event occurred. Arthur Duray in a 110 h.p. Gobron-Brillié (the car with two pistons in each cylinder, mentioned in Chapter 5) achieved the dreamed-of 'ton'. The world record was set at just over 100 m.p.h. for the flying kilometre. 'The Age of the Titans' as this period of racing has been called was there until Bugatti sounded the death knell of the great racers at the French Grand Prix of 1911.

Other important sporting events at this time were the American Vanderbilt Cup, already mentioned in the last chapter, and the Grand Prix, first organized by the Automobile Club de France in 1906. Further signs of the loss of French supremacy appeared in 1907 and 1908. In 1907 the Italians won with a giant F.I.A.T. racer and the following year a German Mercedes was the victor.

Motor racing was, of course, totally prohibited in England. Twenty miles an hour was the maximum speed permitted on the open road. It is paradoxical that it was in England that the greatest motor racing circuit of all was built. William Boddy, the present editor of *Motor Sport*, has written of Brooklands in *Fifty Years of Brooklands* edited by C. Gardner, 'It had an active life of less than thirty years, but they were to be years of adventure, history and incidents the like of which cannot be matched by any other patch of ground in the wide world.' Thus in the country which had prohibited speed the greatest speed track of all sprang up in 1907. But Brooklands was no mere speed track. It was to become the motor laboratory of England and indeed of the world. Cars could be tested there as they could be tested nowhere else. Laurence Pomeroy refers to 'the construction of a 2·73-mile banked concrete circuit south of London by Mr. H. F. Locke-King, in the garden of his house at Weybridge—which was called Brooklands'. In his garden! and incidentally at his own expense—Brooklands cost a quarter of a million to build, the equivalent of about two million today—Hugh Locke-King undertook this massive building operation. William Boddy describes

1. 3½ h.p. Benz of 1898 accompanied by tricycle of the period

2. The first four-wheeled Daimler of 1886—note how similar the arrangement of the front wheels is to that of a bicycle

3. The first Benz motorized tricycle of 1885

4. Close-up view of the Benz engine showing the single open cylinder, the carburettor and the chain drive to rear wheels

5. The great 1901 Mercedes

6. The 1894 Panhard with Daimler engine

7 A 1901 Benz in the 1931 Brighton Run

8. An original picture of Butler's Petrol-cycle displayed with specifications

9. Lord Montagu's father taking King Edward VII (then Prince of Wales) for the first royal drive in a German-built 12 h.p. Daimler

10. 1897 Lanchester, the first four-wheeled British motor car

11. The original Rolls-Royce Silver Ghost which completed a 15,000 mile running test under R.A.C. observation and has now covered half a million miles

12. 1905 Wolseley designed by Herbert Austin—note unusual radiator design which is characteristic of early Wolseleys

13. Assembling the first Rover car in 1904

14. Two early Standard cars of 1908 and 1907

15. An early three-wheeler—Percy Riley's tricar of 1904

16. A highly developed Edwardian three-wheeler—the Morgan of 1913 based on his original of 1909

17. Mr. and Mrs. Henry Ford in the first Ford car of 1896

18. Henry Ford in early Model A

19. Early assembly line for the flywheel-magneto of the Model-T Ford

20. 'Meteor of Road and Track'—*The Autocar*'s description of S. F. Edge's Napier gaining the 24 hour record at Brooklands in 1907

21. Rear view of 120 h.p. racing Itala which can still be seen in the Montagu Motor Museum

22. Jack Johnson, the famous negro boxer, in one of the six-cylinder Austins built for the 1908 French Grand Prix

23. 1910 15 h.p. Austin 'Ascot' two-seater phaeton

24. A British Daimler of around 1911

25. 1913 Chater-Lea as it was when Charlie Russett of Southampton bought it from local gypsies

26. The same car after Mr. Russett's restoration

27. William Morris seated at the wheel of his first Bullnose Morris about to start on the London to Edinburgh run of 1913

Brooklands and the Dawn of Motor Racing

the event, 'During the autumn of 1906 hundreds of workmen had uprooted trees and levelled the ground, using steam grabs, a steam digger and six locomotives, running over seven miles of railway line, while two hundred carpenters erected sheds and shelters.' The River Wey was spanned by the first ferro-concrete bridge of its kind in the world. Against terrible difficulties and opposition from authorities and local people Locke-King fought until finally the Motor Course was completed.

The first event on the course itself was the great designer S. F. Edge's successful attempt to win the twenty-four hours record in the 60 h.p. Napier shown in Plate 20. You must remember that Edge undertook this venture in what was the normal Napier touring car sold to the public and that the year was 1907. In the course of twenty-four hours he covered 1,581 miles, 1,310 yards at an average speed of 65·9 m.p.h. It was a fantastic achievement and one that motoring enthusiasts will always remember. He started his run at 6 o'clock in the evening so that he didn't have to start the night off tired. Once again I have to turn to Boddy's vivid description of the scene: 'As darkness closed over the Track, hundreds of lanterns were lit round its edge and flares spurted and sizzled at the top of the bankings, reflecting weird shadows from the fir trees.' The event shook the motoring world. It also shook the freshly laid concrete of Brooklands and was blamed for much of the later deterioration in the track surface.

Speed records of all kinds were constantly being broken at Brooklands but it was the cars and the men who made the real story of this magnificent and unique motor circuit. In order to get to know more of this early period of racing you should look really carefully at some of the giant racing cars of the day. Two can easily be seen in the Montagu Motor Museum: the massive 1907 120 h.p. Itala (Plate 21) and the 1908 Grand Prix Austin (Plate 22). Note the great area of the big flat-fronted radiators. The concept of streamlining had not yet emerged. In one respect the two racers in the Museum differ from most of the other giants of the day, the Mercedes, F.I.A.T. and Panhard, in that they have live rear axles and not chain and sprocket for the final drive.

By 1908 and 1909 speeds were well over the 100 mile an hour mark

Brooklands and the Dawn of Motor Racing

but small cars and production models were also given their chance. Races were arranged for all categories of cars and Test Hill was built at Brooklands to try their hill-climbing capacities. Challenges were issued by manufacturers. Both research and publicity played a very important part in the variety of sporting events which were being developed at Brooklands, and a strain of envy was creeping into the comments of foreign motoring journals when they spoke of the great British autodrome.

The years from 1910 to 1914 were used extensively for research at Brooklands. It did for motoring what the roads of France had done during the Veteran period. Boddy tells us, 'Two particularly outstanding cars enlivened the 1909 season. One of them was a specially slim, single-seater Vauxhall, sharply tapering back and front, its radiator cowl having an opening merely $2\frac{1}{2}$ inches wide, and with discs covering its wheels.' The value of streamlining was beginning to be realized and new shapes were soon to dominate the scene. This Vauxhall called 'KN' (because it was as hot as Cayenne pepper) started a new fashion in narrow, streamlined, single-seater Brooklands racers. The other car was a massive 84·8 h.p., chain-driven Benz. It attacked records with a vengeance and was electrically timed at 128 m.p.h. over the half-mile.

Louis Coatalen, the great Sunbeam designer, was also experimenting with streamlining, paving the way to the great speed record breakers of the Vintage period. Crowds were becoming large and the names of the famous Brooklands drivers were emerging with colourful nicknames for the cars that accompanied them: Percy Lambert with his Austin 'Pearley', Louis Coatalen in his Sunbeam 'Toddles II', Malcolm Campbell in his Darracq 'The Flapper'. Brooklands built a whole social life around car racing, but the hard plodding of the mechanics and the serious research of the designers were always in the background, nor was tragedy absent. Narrow shaves were numerous. A Mercedes managed to strip some of the spokes from the wheel of a Napier which it was overtaking and thus provided thrills for the crowd. Perhaps the most amusing incident was when the popular driver, 'Cupid' Hornsted, after sliding 100 yards sideways and spinning round three times, flew into the evil-smelling sewage farm behind the track.

In 1910 Vauxhalls coaxed 100 m.p.h. out of a 21 h.p. car and in the

Brooklands and the Dawn of Motor Racing

following year 98 m.p.h. from only 16 h.p. In 1912 Malcolm Campbell almost met his end when both his off-side wheels collapsed simultaneously. 'Sliding along on its hubs amid showers of sparks and clouds of cement dust, the car tore down the iron railings as if they had been matchsticks.' Campbell stepped out unhurt. In 1913 Percy Lambert set the World's Hour Record at 103·84 m.p.h., the first time that more than 100 miles had been covered in 60 minutes. Shortly after it was taken by a Peugeot of nearly twice the engine capacity and in trying to wrest it back Percy Lambert, one of the greatest stars of Brooklands, died.

Perhaps you have gained a taste for the exciting events which occurred on that great racing circuit and want to know more. William Boddy has written three extensive volumes on events at which he himself was frequently present. They are crammed with facts and highly technical. It would be better to start with the same author's much shorter account in *Fifty Years of Brooklands* edited by Gardner, from which I have quoted. You will really enjoy that and not find it too hard to read.

While all this was going on at Brooklands, racing abroad, of course, did not stop. In the 1911 Grand Prix Bugatti achieved his remarkable success with his little Type 13 and in the following year a Peugeot with overhead-camshaft engine actually won, beating all the giant racers with engines twice the size of its own. The clouds of war, however, were hanging over all racing. Brooklands was handed over to the Royal Flying Corps and many of the great car firms on both sides turned to the manufacture of aircraft engines. The significance of aerial warfare was suddenly realized and the great designers turned their attention to producing light powerful engines to hurtle across the sky.

8 · A Final Survey of the Edwardian Scene

The last few years before the First World War contained the Vintage scene in embryo. Almost all the well-known makes of that period had emerged and many were already famous. Herbert Austin was well known for his work with Wolseley as well as his various attempts in the field of racing. He had produced a little 7 h.p. tourer on the Swift design as well as a large tourer which was to pave the way to his sturdy cars of the Vintage period (Plate 23). Singer, Standard and Vauxhall were very firmly established indeed. Vauxhall's famous 'Prince Henry' (named after Prince Henry of Prussia) 20 h.p. C-Type has been described by Lord Montagu as the world's first true sports car. It is a car that sporting fans need to look at very closely and there are two slightly later models in the Montagu Motor Museum with the larger 25 h.p. engine.

21. 1912 Turner, light car of the late Edwardian period

A Final Survey of the Edwardian Scene

Unlike most of the successful Brooklands cars the C-Type seemed just as suited to taking the family out on a quiet Sunday afternoon, such was its remarkable versatility. The Turner of 1912 illustrated a typical light car of the age. In 1913 the four-cylinder A.C. appeared, merely to be submerged for the War and to reappear prominently in the Vintage period. But perhaps the most significant venture of all was the building of the first Bullnose Morris Oxford by William Morris, a bicycle manufacturer (Plate 27). Here was the first of an astounding line of mass-produced cars which were to tear the bottom out of the market of their competitors and blaze the way towards popular motoring. The story of how Morris and Austin followed the example set by Henry Ford is a Vintage story and must be left to that period. One of the greatest changes in car design is very evident in the 1914 45 h.p. Napier

22. 45 h.p. Napier Pullman showing the shape of things to come

Pullman Limousine. The long low bonnet and the low bodywork show that even the designers of closed cars had at last got away from the last traces of the old horse carriages. The problems of scaling down this kind of design to suit the light car remained over to be tackled during the 'twenties.

A Final Survey of the Edwardian Scene

Perhaps too little has been said about the refinements in motoring which have now become almost inseparable in our minds from the concept of the motor car. The need for all-weather protection had grown as the car came to be regarded as an essential part of the transport system of the nation. Lights too were not a primary concern in the early days but they also came to be seen as essential. Oil lamps and crude acetylene gas lamps were the only means of illumination. They flickered and frequently blew out on windy nights and after every night journey they involved the driver in a complicated process of cleaning when his eyes were tired and he probably felt like sinking into bed. By the end of the Edwardian period clean simple electric lighting had become almost universal. The invention of the detachable wheel rim helped to avoid the unpleasantness of taking out inner tubes and mending punctures by the roadside. But by the end of the period this had given way to the even simpler detachable wheel such as we still use today. The electric self-starter had also come into wide use and any older motorist who has had trouble with his starter motor will tell you how much this little device means to him as a motorist.

The days of gleaming brass were fading and signs of the emergence of a much more utilitarian kind of car were plain. Soon, for better or for worse, the motor car was to become the accepted means of transport for a vast number of families. A great pioneering age was over, an age when men had wrestled in the dark with the imponderable alternatives of engine design and body construction and layout. Civilization lurched forward hundreds of years in a fraction of a century. Without doubt the motor car led the rapid march into mechanization, on the road, in the air, in war and in peace. Many of us take all this so much for granted that we laugh at the 'old crocks' made by the brilliant pioneers of motoring. It is they who should be alive now to laugh at us for failing to grasp the shattering importance of the history of the motor car.

9 · *Museums, Clubs and Events You Should Know About*

The aim of this book could never have been to introduce you to the vast panorama of individual cars which were made in the Veteran and Edwardian periods. Nor is it meant to be a mere pocket-book of old cars. It is as a guide to the remarkable growth of the motor car that it comes to you, to give the feel of a brief age that brought the car into being. This happened by fast, stumbling steps and each new advance was not simply a single step forward for a particular make but is significant as part of a great organism that was to disrupt the pattern of life which had gone on for centuries. To know the facts and to sense the meaning behind a mystery which had eluded man for countless centuries must be the aims of the aspiring expert. It is to start you along these lines that this book is designed. It is to help you help yourself. Veteran and Edwardian cars are by no means so active as those of the Vintage era. They are rare and exorbitantly valuable. The occasion when they do really come out in force is the London to Brighton Run held on the first Sunday in November every year. To see this is a 'must' for every Veteran car enthusiast. It is a veritable museum in action. The great museums can also help you to understand man's struggle to create automotive power. The Montagu Motor Museum at Beaulieu in Hampshire must surely be known to everyone whether they have an interest in Veteran cars or not. It was founded by Lord Montagu of Beaulieu in 1952 in memory of his father, who was one of the great pioneers of motoring and a champion of the motor car in Parliament through all the early struggles to get it accepted in this country. The Montagu Motor Museum is open all the year round, and if you take a look at the calendar of events in the *Veteran and Vintage Magazine* you can arrange your visit to coincide with one of the many specialist rallies which happen to interest you. Cars are constantly going in and out of this museum and the sound of revving historic engines is never long absent around Beaulieu. It is a living museum and aims to keep Veteran,

Museums, Clubs and Events You Should Know About

Edwardian and Vintage days alive in every possible way. The Science Museum in South Kensington is another very exciting place for the Veteran enthusiast. Some of the very early cars are well placed for you to look closely into their works and the excellent illuminated displays of the electrical ignition system and the vaporizing function of the carburettor will help to increase your knowledge of how the car works.

Other collections are small by comparison with these two internationally famous museums. The Shuttleworth Collection, consisting mainly of aeroplanes which are frequently displayed, has also a few very interesting early cars and is well worth a visit. It is at the Old Warden Aerodrome at Biggleswade in Bedfordshire. There is also the Veteran Car Club Museum at Cheddar in Somerset.

In addition to all these larger collections, however, it is well worth remembering that many garages and car showrooms have the odd early car tucked away, which their owners are ready to tell you about in order to stimulate interest in the make which they are actually selling. Private people with Veteran and Edwardian cars also exist around the country and their owners usually respond to enthusiasm on the part of young people, especially if they show they have taken trouble to obtain some knowledge on the subject. An afternoon spent nosing around the garages of your town or city can often be very rewarding. The scrap yards are seldom worth visiting these days although I did recently visit one myself and discovered among the undergrowth behind it an early Model T Ford with a small tree growing up through the chassis!

The Veteran Car Club of Great Britain organizes many events and has done sterling work from the earliest days to preserve our motoring heritage, but it is rather an exclusive club and perhaps cannot in the nature of things be so active as the Vintage Sports Car Club. Even for Edwardian car enthusiasts the V.S.C.C. can be very helpful, for among the various early racing cars driven at its various annual events on the great racing circuits there are usually several of the great monster racers of the Edwardian era blasting their mighty way round the track, notably Cecil Clutton's Itala.

Although most of the Veteran and many of the Edwardian cars are hardly everyday practical propositions, the tremendous quality of these

Museums, Clubs and Events You Should Know About

cars: the solid brass, the top-quality steel, the pioneering attitudes of the men who built them, the strokes of engineering genius in them, the lifetime of patient experiment which made some working part possible, the fact that they were not built down to a price, these are the things that will always endear them to us.

Some Other Books to Read

Many of these books are highly technical. You may want some of them only for reference and to understand some you may need help from a really knowledgeable person. Books like those of Laurence Pomeroy on motor racing history you will find very exciting if you skip some of the extremely technical passages and pick out the story. Here then are a few books of special interest:

L. T. C. Rolt, *Motoring History*, Studio Vista (a good general account of the whole history of motoring).

Peter Roberts, *Veteran and Vintage Cars*, Paul Hamlyn (a good picture story book).

A. Bird and F. Hutton-Scott, *The Veteran Motor Car Pocketbook*, Batsford (excellent for identification purposes and for checking technical details).

Lord Montagu, *Lost Causes of Motoring*, Cassell (some out-of-the-ordinary information).

Lord Montagu, *Lost Causes of Motoring: Europe*, Cassell (more out-of-the-ordinary information).

Lord Montagu, *The Motoring Montagus*, Cassell (contains an excellent account of the early struggles of the motorist as well as the story of the Montagu Motor Museum. Out of print but obtainable from libraries).

Peter Hull, *History of the Vintage Sports-Car Club*, Cassell (contains quite a bit about Edwardian racers and sporting-type cars).

J. D. Scheel, *Cars of the World*, Methuen (excellent handbook with very wide coverage).

For those with a special interest in racing and sports cars there are the following books:

C. Gardner (ed.), *Fifty Years of Brooklands*, Heinemann (read W. Boddy's section on cars).

W. Boddy, *History of Brooklands Motor Course*, H. Marshall and Son (for a full and technical account).

David McDonald, *Fifty Years with the Speed Kings*, Stanley Paul.

Some Other Books to Read

L. Pomeroy, *The Evolution of the Racing Car*, William Kimber.
L. Pomeroy, *The Grand Prix Car*, Motor Racing Publications Ltd.

For those who wish to gain a quick and simple idea of the mechanisms of motor cars in order to further their understanding of the early cars with which this book deals there is:

Harry Heywood and Patrick Macnaghten, *Your Book about the Way a Car Works*, Faber and Faber.

The Profile Publications give very worthwhile and comprehensive accounts of individual cars, and *The Veteran and Vintage Magazine* is a general monthly publication which the Veteran and early motor car enthusiast can scarcely afford to miss. In addition to these the catalogues of both the Montagu Motor Museum and the Science Museum are excellent sources of information about cars in those museums.

Index

A.C., 36, 53
Adler, 41
Alldays and Onions, 29
Austin, 32, 33, 37, 49, 50, 52
Austin, Sir Herbert, 32, 36, 46, 47, 52, 53
Automobile Association, 35

Benz cars, 13, 17, 28, 41, 43, 45, 49
Benz, Karl, 15, 16, 17, 18, 19
Boddy, William, 48, 49, 50, 51
Bollée, 20, 39
Bouton, Georges, 23
Brooklands, 48, 49, 50, 51, 53
Bugatti cars, 41
Bugatti, Ettore, 39, 41, 48, 51
Buick, 46
Butler, Edward, 27

Cadillac, 45, 46
Calthorpe, 35, 36
Campbell, Malcolm, 50, 51
Chevrolet, 46
Coatalen, Louis, 50
Cugnot, Nicholas Joseph, 11, 12

Daimler, Gottlieb, 15, 16, 18, 19, 20, 21, 24
Daimler cars, 15, 17, 25, 28, 29
Darracq, 39, 50
Decauville, 30, 40
de Dion Bouton cars, 23, 24
de Dion, Count Albert, 20, 21, 23
Delage, 39
Delahaye, 39
Delaunay-Belleville, 40
Dunlop, John Boyd, 22

Duray, Arthur, 48
Duryea Brothers, 42

Edge, S. F., 47, 49

Fiat, 41, 48, 49
Ford cars, 14, 43, 44, 56
Ford, Henry, 14, 18, 43, 44, 45, 46, 53

General Motors, 45
Genevieve, 23, 40
Gobron-Brillié, 39, 40, 48
Gordon Bennett Trophy, 30, 47
Grand Prix, 48, 51

Hot tube ignition, 17, 22
Humber, 30, 34, 46

Internal combustion engine, 12
Itala, 49, 56

Jellinek, Mercedes, 19
Johnson, Claude, 30, 31
Jowett, 36

King Edward VII, 14, 28
Knight, J. H., 27, 28

Lagonda, 36
Lambert, Percy, 50, 51
Lanchester cars, 28, 37
Lanchester, Frederick, 28
Lea-Francis, 36
Levassor, Emile, 20, 21, 24, 25, 32
Light Locomotives Act, 12, 26, 27, 28
'Live' rear axle, 22, 30

61

Index

Locke-King, F. H., 48, 49
Locomobile, 46
London to Brighton Run, 13, 27, 55

Macadam, 13
Marcus, Siegfried, 15, 16, 20, 27
Maybach, Wilhelm, 16, 18, 19, 22
Mercedes, 19, 30, 41, 48, 49, 50
Mercedes-Benz, 19
Mercer, 46
Michelin Brothers, 22
Montagu, Lord, 13, 28, 52, 55
Montagu Motor Museum, 13, 23, 27, 31, 33, 34, 46, 49, 52, 55
Morgan, H. F. S., 37
Morris Oxford (Bullnose), 53
Morris, William, 37, 46, 53
Mors, 39, 47
Motor Show, 26

Napier cars, 28, 30, 37, 47, 49, 50, 53
Napier, Montague, 30
Newcomen, Thomas, 11
N.S.U., 41

Oakland, 46
Oldsmobile, 45
Opel, 41
Otto Cycle, 16
Otto, N. A., 16

Panhard cars, 22, 24, 38, 39, 41, 47, 49
Paris to Bordeaux Race, 22, 24
Paris to Madrid Race, 47
Paris to Marseilles Race, 25
Paris to Rouen Race, 24
Pennington Autocar, 46
Peugeot, 22, 39, 41, 51
Pomeroy, Laurence, 47, 48

Red Flag Act, see Light Locomotives Act
Renault cars, 23, 28, 38, 39
Renault, Louis, 22, 23, 34, 39, 47
Rocket, 11
Rolls, C. S., 28, 30, 31, 38
Rolls-Royce cars, 30, 31, 32, 37
Rolt, L. T. C., 41
Rover, 30, 34
Royal Automobile Club, 28
Royce, F. H., 30, 31, 37, 40

Salomons, Sir David, 26
Sarazin, Eduard, 20
Science Museum, 17, 18, 22, 31, 56
Serpollet, Léon, 20, 21
Shuttleworth Collection, 56
Singer, 52
Spyker, 23, 40
Standard, 36, 52
Star, 28, 37
Stephenson, George, 11
Sunbeam, 33, 37, 50
Système Panhard et Levassor, 20, 21, 22, 39, 45

Thousand Mile Round Britain Trial, 28, 30
Triumph, 28, 37
Turner, 53

Vanderbilt Cup, 46, 48
Vauxhall, 34, 35, 49, 50, 52
Veteran Car Club of Great Britain, 56
Veteran Car Club Museum, 56
Vintage Sports Car Club, 56

Watt, James, 11
Winton, Alexander, 43
Wolseley cars, 28, 32, 37, 47
Wolseley–Siddeley, 36